Not Just Dirt!

HOW SOIL SUPPORTS OUR PLANET

SHERYL NORMANDEAU

ORCA BOOK PUBLISHERS

Published in Canada and the United States in 2025 by Orca Book Publishers.
orcabook.com

Library and Archives Canada Cataloguing in Publication
Title: Not just dirt! : how soil supports our planet / Sheryl Normandeau.
Names: Normandeau, Sheryl, author
Series: Orca footprints ; 35.
Description: Series statement: Orca footprints ; 35 | Includes bibliographical references and index.
Identifiers: Canadiana (print) 20240461290 | Canadiana (ebook) 20240461304 |
ISBN 9781459839755 (hardcover) | ISBN 9781459839731 (PDF) | ISBN 9781459839748 (EPUB)
Subjects: LCSH: Soils—Juvenile literature. | LCSH: Soils—Environmental aspects—Juvenile literature. |
LCSH: Soil conservation—Juvenile literature. | LCGFT: Informational works.
Classification: LCC S596 .N67 2025 | DDC j631.4—dc23

Library of Congress Control Number: 2024946224

Summary: Part of the nonfiction Orca Footprints series for middle-grade readers and illustrated with color photographs throughout, this book explores the importance of soil to all life on Earth and how we can conserve it for the future.

Orca Book Publishers is committed to reducing the consumption of nonrenewable resources in the production of our books. We make every effort to use materials that support a sustainable future.

Orca Book Publishers gratefully acknowledges the support for its publishing programs provided by the following agencies: the Government of Canada, the Canada Council for the Arts and the Province of British Columbia through the BC Arts Council and the Book Publishing Tax Credit.

Front cover photos by Viorika/Getty Images and Jessie Casson/Getty Images.
Back cover photos by Mint Images/Getty Images, Westend61/Getty Images and Marcel ter Bekke/Getty Images.
Design by Dahlia Yuen.
Edited by Kirstie Hudson.

Printed and bound in South Korea.

28 27 26 25 • 1 2 3 4

To all the soil builders and seed sowers—you are needed.

What would our world look like without soil? Well, it definitely wouldn't be filled with green plants!
ANDRESWD/GETTY IMAGES

Contents

CHAPTER THREE: SOIL UNDER THREAT

CHAPTER FOUR: HEALTHY SOIL FOR THE FUTURE

Introduction

Nothing beats getting your hands into the soil and growing some plants! The potatoes in my community garden bed will end up on my supper plate very soon.
ROB NORMANDEAU

I love to garden. When I pull a big, juicy carrot out of my garden bed and take a crunchy bite, I know the reason that carrot is so tasty has a lot to do with the soil it grew in. Because my garden soil is healthy, it is full of nutrients and life. There are earthworms in the soil, feeding on dead leaves and other organic matter. Bacteria, fungi and other microorganisms are also in the soil, breaking down plant and animal waste and composting them. My carrots receive nutrients from these processes. The soil also holds water so that my carrots can use it when they need it.

We don't always think about the importance of soil, but can you imagine a world without it? Farmers grow crops such as wheat, barley, oats, corn and peas in soil. We mine the soil for resources that we use in manufacturing and for fuel. Soil is used in the construction of roads and buildings. It provides food and habitat for animals that live both underground and above ground.

Soil may support the planet, but problems caused by human activity have a massive impact on soil health. Pollution, deforestation and the climate crisis are destroying soil at an alarming rate. This could harm all life on Earth. Although governments and organizations are working to preserve soil health, and are using new technologies and methods to harvest resources without damaging soil, there is much we can do on our own to help. If we all work together, we can make sure our soil is healthy for the future. Are you ready to dig in and learn more?

Gardening at school is one way to learn about soil and how it supports plant life—plus, you can eat the vegetables you grow!

ALISTAIR BERG/GETTY IMAGES

CHAPTER ONE

What on Earth Is Soil?

SVYATOSLAV BALAN/GETTY IMAGES

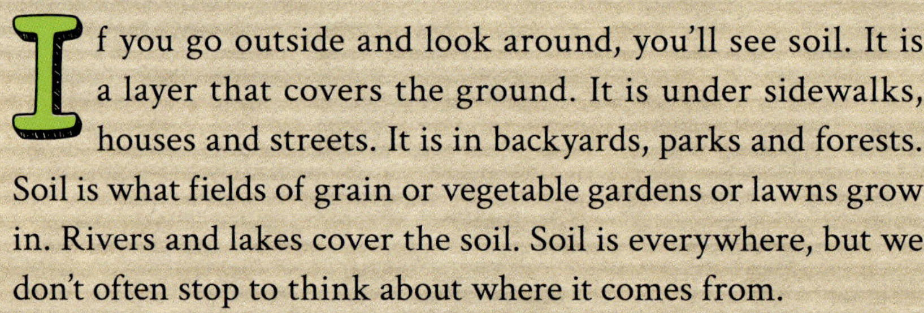

If you go outside and look around, you'll see soil. It is a layer that covers the ground. It is under sidewalks, houses and streets. It is in backyards, parks and forests. Soil is what fields of grain or vegetable gardens or lawns grow in. Rivers and lakes cover the soil. Soil is everywhere, but we don't often stop to think about where it comes from.

SOIL'S ORIGIN STORY

Soil is made from rocks. The rocks contain many different minerals. Soil is formed when the rocks are broken down, or ***eroded***, by water, wind and frost. This is called physical weathering. Rocks can also break down due to chemical weathering. This happens when minerals inside the rocks have a chemical reaction to water or air.

Over thousands of years, rock is worn down to create soil. Water is a type of erosion agent.
SHERYL NORMANDEAU

If you've ever been hiking in the mountains, you may have seen how tree roots can split open rocks. This is biological weathering—a living organism has caused the rock to break. Chemical and biological weathering are not as common as physical weathering.

Because different types of rocks exist all over the world, the soils created from them are also different. Soils are unique. Limestone will create a different type of soil than granite or basalt. Layers of soil called horizons make up what is called the soil profile. Soil profiles are different all over the planet.

Time—a lot of it!—is needed to make soil. It can take up to tens of thousands of years for rock to erode into soil. A hot, wet climate can make the process go more quickly than a dry, cold climate.

Even mountains break down over time—a *lot* of time! Sometimes tree roots can crack rocks. Other times running water or snowfall causes rockslides.

SHERYL NORMANDEAU

Soil contains a few more ingredients besides rocks and minerals. It is also made up of **air**, **water**, **organic matter** such as dead plants and animals, and an abundance of **living organisms**.

BEAVERA/GETTY IMAGES

Birds such as this chickadee eat insects found in the soil or in trees that grow in soil.
SHERYL NORMANDEAU

SOIL AND PLANT LIFE

Imagine your life without soil. From the house you live in to the clothes you wear and the food you eat, soil plays an important role. Soil supports plants and trees of all kinds by holding their root systems in place. Soil also provides nutrients, water and air to plants. Plants are used by humans for fiber, clothing, food, medicine and more. Plants are also used by animals, birds and insects for food, habitat and raising their offspring. Soil is also the foundation for our buildings and our roads—without it, it would be very difficult to support the world's population.

WORKING TOGETHER

Fungi have a special relationship with soil and plants. They all work together to share and transport nutrients and water.
KICHIGIN/GETTY IMAGES

Mycorrhiza is a partnership between tree roots and some types of fungi. These fungi have thin, threadlike "roots" called mycelium. The mycelium wrap around tree roots and connect with other fungi and trees in the forest. In this way, the fungi can help deliver nutrients and water to the trees. The fungi can't ***photosynthesize,*** so they can't manufacture carbohydrates, which they need. The trees can supply that for them.

LENSBLUR/GETTY IMAGES

KADMY/GETTY IMAGES

What Does a Geotechnical Engineer Do?

Before a building is constructed, a geotechnical engineer is consulted to find out if the site is safe to build on. Geotechnical engineers collect samples of soil and rock and analyze data about construction sites. They look for potential hazards, such as landslides. Geotechnical engineers work with architects as well as the construction team to ensure that the rocks and soil are a good match for the project.

KALI9/GETTY IMAGES

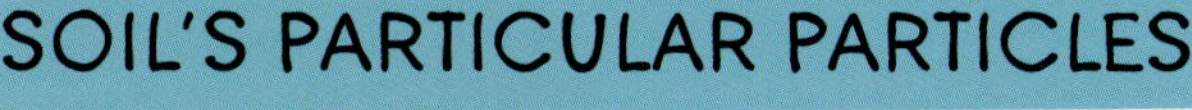

SOIL'S PARTICULAR PARTICLES

Soil is made up of sand, silt and clay particles. These particles create the texture of the soil. Soil with coarse (large) particles, such as sand, allows water and nutrients to run through it easily. This means that sandy soils dry out quickly and don't hold nutrients for very long. One benefit of sandy soils is that they are easy to dig into. Clay, on the other hand, has a very fine texture. Soil with a lot of clay particles can hold water and nutrients, but it is hard to dig. Water doesn't easily run through clay soil, and sometimes water can pool on top of the soil. Different plants grow in different types of soil. Some, like many types of cacti, like sandy soil. They don't need a lot of water and nutrients to survive. Other plants, like willow trees, like wet soil. They can handle soil with more clay in it.

WESTEND61/GETTY IMAGES

Feeling Happy

A bacteria found in soil called *Mycobacterium vaccae* can make us happier! Studies show that exposure to *M. vaccae* can increase the level of a neurotransmitter called serotonin in our brains. Serotonin is a mood stabilizer and can help us deal with stress. It is possible to encounter *M. vaccae* while we are working in the soil in our gardens. It's just one more reason why growing a garden is so good for our health.

The safety of our buildings relies on the structure of the soil and the stability it provides.

BEN-SCHONEWILLE/GETTY IMAGES

CHOOSE WISELY

Knowing the texture of the soil in an area is very important when building houses, roads or other structures. Building on soil that pools with water or shifts over time is dangerous. Landslides or flooding or other disasters could happen. When a road is built, heavy machinery flattens and compacts the soil, making it level. Sometimes a binding agent such as cement or salt is added to the soil to keep it from being loose and soft. When roads are constructed, ditches, culverts and drains are added so that water does not pool on the road and cause problems. The goal is to make sure that the soil can safely support the structure on top of it.

SOIL KEEPS RECORDS OF THE PAST

Soil holds thousands of years of human history by storing artifacts from past civilizations. ***Archaeologists*** sift through the soil to uncover details about our ancestors. From the ruins of the ancient city of Qatna in Syria, the Terracotta Army in China and the maze-like underground complex of Derinkuyu in Türkiye we have a better understanding of where humans have come from because of the relics buried in the soil. Without finding all these places, the past would be forgotten.

One interesting find includes the Jorvik Viking settlement in York, England. The Vikings lived in York around 975. Archaeologists were able to learn a great deal about how the Viking settlers lived because they uncovered items such as shoes, clothing, bones, roof tiles, pottery and even seeds in the ground. Because the soil preserved these important tools and goods from the Vikings' lives, we know more about them.

Soil stores our history! When we unearth artifacts from the soil, we learn about our ancestors and the way they lived.

DAN GABRIEL ATANASIE/SHUTTERSTOCK.COM

Dirt Even Older than Dirt

Paleosols are ancient layers of soil that have been buried by sediments left from floods, volcanoes or landslides. Some of the paleosols that scientists around the world are studying are 2.7 to 2.9 billion years old! By studying paleosols, scientists can discover more about how the climate has changed on Earth over this incredibly long period of time.

THE STORY OF THE PIPESTONE BONEBED

Soil also holds fossils and evidence of plants and animals from millions of years ago. ***Paleontologists*** work to unearth dinosaur bones and other specimens from that time. Scientists have been finding dinosaur fossils in the Pipestone Creek area of northern Alberta since the 1970s, but in 2008 they made a big discovery. They found a large bed containing the fossils of a herd of dinosaur species no one had seen before: *Pachyrhinosaur lakustai*, or thick-nosed lizard (so named because of the big bony bump above the nose and eyes). The bonebed dates to 72.5 million years ago. This incredible find and others—such as the discovery of the bones of a small raptor called *Boreonykus certekorum* in the same area in 2016—are allowing scientists to piece together more information about these fascinating creatures from Earth's past.

There are secrets in the stones! We can unlock the mysteries of ancient plants and animals by looking at fossils that are buried in the soil.
TINA BOISVERT

If you want to know the texture of the soil in your garden, taking soil samples will help you find out.

HAPPYNATI/GETTY IMAGES

LET'S EXPERIMENT: SOIL TEST

There is an easy way to see how much sand, silt and clay particles a sample of soil contains. Grab an empty glass jar out of your recycling bin. Make sure it has a lid. Go out to your garden and put a large scoop of soil into the jar. Fill the jar three-quarters to the top with water and cover the jar tightly with the lid. Shake the jar hard, then put it aside for at least 24 hours.

When you check your soil sample, you'll see that the particles in the soil have settled into three layers in the water. The sand layer will be on the bottom of the jar, because sand particles are large and coarse, and water runs freely through them. The silt layer will be in the middle of the jar. Silt particles are less coarse than sand particles. Clay particles will make up the top layer in the jar. Clay particles are very fine, and water does not go through them easily. Try sampling soil from different areas of your garden. See if you get the same results with each sample.

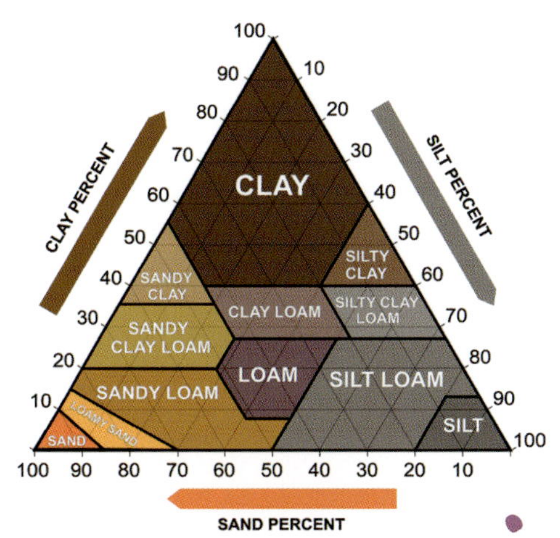

The soil texture triangle is a classification system that tells you what type of soil you have based on the amount of clay, silt and sand the soil contains.

ALI DAMOUH/SCIENCE PHOTO LIBRARY/GETTY IMAGES

What Does Soil Do for Us?

Successful Soil Dwellers

Sow bugs are strange-looking armored creatures that you sometimes see crawling around on dead leaves or wood mulch. They look like insects, but they are not—they are ***crustaceans*** and are related to shrimp and crayfish. They cannot live underwater, though—they are land dwellers. Sow bugs can be found all over the world. They have gills like their aquatic relatives, and they need the soil around them to be damp so that they can breathe. They eat decaying plant matter.

SARAHLUNDPHOTOGRAPHY/GETTY IMAGES

Through technology and science, humans have learned to use soil in many different, often surprising, ways. Soil can help fill our needs and make us healthier. It can also provide some solutions to dealing with environmental problems.

THE WEB OF LIFE IN THE SOIL—WE'RE ALL CONNECTED!

The soil food web is made up of all the organisms that live in the soil. They work together as part of the web. Beneath the soil, where the roots of plants grow, fungi, bacteria and other microorganisms such as protists feast on other microorganisms. Earthworms and insects such as centipedes and springtails work their way through the soil. Some of them eat plant matter,

All types of wildlife—even humans—rely on the soil food web. We are all connected by our interactions with soil.

SHERYL NORMANDEAU

FRANCISCO MARTINS/GETTY IMAGES

MONCHERIE/GETTY IMAGES

SANTIAGO URQUIJO/GETTY IMAGES

CHRIS STEIN/GETTY IMAGES

while others eat other insects. Larger animals that make their homes in the soil, such as moles and voles, eat plants and insects. Aboveground, deer, mice, rabbits, squirrels, birds and other wildlife eat a buffet of fruit, leaves, seeds, insects and other animals. Pollinating insects, birds and bats help plants form fruit, nuts and seeds. If you grow vegetables and other edible plants, you can enjoy the bounty of your harvest on the dinner table. The scraps from your meal can be used to make compost and go back into the soil. And the web keeps going!

THE STORY OF PENICILLIN

Penicillin, the first ***antibiotic***, was discovered in 1928 by Dr. Alexander Fleming, in London, England. Before that time, there were no antibiotics to treat infections such as blood poisoning and meningitis. Many people died from illnesses that we can treat today with antibiotics.

Antibiotics are made from ***beneficial*** bacteria or fungi. They work to destroy harmful bacteria or fungi or prevent them from harming people. In Fleming's original experiment, he found a special type of mold growing in a petri dish full of *Staphylococcus* bacteria. The mold seemed to be preventing the

A DOUBT/WIKIMEDIA COMMONS/CC BY-SA 4.0

Alexander Fleming works in his laboratory in 1943.

IMPERIAL WAR MUSEUM/WIKIMEDIA COMMONS/PUBLIC DOMAIN

harmful bacteria from growing. That mold contained a genus of fungus called *Penicillium*, which is commonly found in soil. Fleming published a report of his findings in 1929. He and his colleagues spent years doing further experiments, without much success.

In 1939 researchers at Oxford University began doing ***clinical trials*** to ensure the drug made from the fungus would work on humans. Eventually they were successful. By this time World War II had begun, and scientists wanted to get supplies of penicillin to British soldiers on the battlefield to help treat wounds and infections such as pneumonia. But it was difficult to produce enough of the drug to help everyone. In 1941 Britain and the United States started working together to boost the production of the antibiotic. By the end of the war, penicillin was widely used in the military. After the war, ***pharmaceutical*** companies were chosen to produce and market the drug to civilians. Today penicillin is one of the most common antibiotics used in the world.

Penicillin and other antibiotics can help people fight many different types of illness.
ONFOKUS/GETTY IMAGES

SOIL BACTERIA GIVE ANTIBIOTICS A BOOST

Penicillin does not work to fight off all infectious bacteria. Over time some diseases have become ***resistant*** to the antibiotic. This happens because some bacteria ***mutate***. They can adapt to protect themselves against antibiotics such as penicillin. Researchers are looking into ways to make antibiotics more capable of fighting off these so-called superbugs. Some bacteria found in soil make a compound called tunicamycin. When tunicamycin is used with penicillin, it appears to make the antibiotic stronger and more effective in fighting off some infections. More studies need to be done, but one day tunicamycin and other soil bacteria may be used to give antibiotics a boost.

In the future there may be additional ways that soil can help make our medicines better.
KITREEL/SHUTTERSTOCK.COM

JANIECBROS/GETTY IMAGES

Giving Farmers Credit

Some farmers try to reduce the amount of carbon dioxide that is released into the atmosphere by not tilling their land. No-till farming involves putting the seeds into holes drilled into the earth, an approach that doesn't disturb the soil. In some parts of the world, farmers have the option of participating in carbon offset or carbon credit programs. Corporations or companies, such as manufacturers that process iron and steel, produce a lot of carbon that goes into the atmosphere. The government will allow these companies to purchase carbon credits (which are like a coupon) from farmers. That means the corporations can keep producing atmospheric carbon, while the farmers store enough carbon in the soil to make up for the amount that is being emitted into the atmosphere. It's a bit like balancing on a teeter-totter!

USDA NATURAL RESOURCES CONSERVATION SERVICE/ WIKIMEDIA COMMONS/PUBLIC DOMAIN

CAN SOIL HELP WITH THE CLIMATE CRISIS?

Greenhouse gases such as carbon dioxide that are trapped in Earth's atmosphere are causing massive changes to the planet's climate. Carbon dioxide can sit in the atmosphere for thousands of years. This means that global warming will continue to worsen unless humans reduce greenhouse gas emissions. Another strategy is to store carbon dioxide emissions in places where it will not be able to escape into the atmosphere. Soil is one of these places. (Oceans and forests are others.) Soil stores up to three times as much carbon dioxide as the atmosphere.

HOW DOES CARBON STORAGE WORK?

Plants contain carbon, as does every living thing. Plant roots grow deep below the surface of the soil. When a plant dies, the roots decompose underground, and the carbon in them stays in the soil. It isn't released into the atmosphere.

If we want to prevent the carbon deep in the soil from being disturbed and released into the atmosphere, we need to find alternatives to practices like deep tilling (digging up) farmland. Unfortunately, tillage is part of large-scale agriculture all over the world.

Changing some of the ways we use farm equipment to work the soil may improve soil health.

OTICKI/GETTY IMAGES

Metals such as copper are extracted from open pit mines like this.
MATTGUSH/GETTY IMAGES

MINING THE EARTH

Soil contains minerals and other resources that we can mine and use in manufacturing, industry, construction and our everyday lives.

Gypsum
This mineral is used to make drywall, which is found in homes mostly in North America.

Copper
Wire and pipes made of copper are used for electrical work and plumbing—and copper is also in computer chips.

Aluminum
Soda is consumed by people all around the world, and the cans are made from the mineral aluminum. Frying pans are also commonly made from aluminum.

Graphite
The mineral graphite is used to make fishing rods, golf clubs, lubricants and pencil leads.

A: WITT CAMERAMAN/SHUTTERSTOCK.COM; POTASHEV ALEKSANDR/SHUTTERSTOCK.COM
B: ZELENSKAYA/SHUTTERSTOCK.COM; FABRIKASIMF/SHUTTERSTOCK.COM
C: RHJPHTOTOS/SHUTTERSTOCK.COM; FABRIKASIMF/SHUTTERSTOCK.COM
D: BJOERN WYLEZICH/SHUTTERSTOCK.COM; NEW AFRICA/SHUTTERSTOCK.COM

Helium-filled balloons are often given as gifts at birthdays, but helium has a lot of practical uses too. It's used in MRI examinations of the lungs and other organs. Researchers are examining ways helium might help patients with respiratory diseases. Helium is also used to cool nuclear reactors and rockets. It might surprise you to know that most of the helium on the planet is found in Earth's crust. It is often ***extracted*** from the soil alongside natural gas.

VOVANTARAKAN/SHUTTERSTOCK.COM
VLADI333/SHUTTERSTOCK.COM

Many of the minerals found in soil are needed for human health. Plants take up minerals when they grow in soil that contains minerals. When humans eat those plants, such as potatoes and beans, they will also ingest some of the minerals that were in the soil. Livestock such as cattle might also eat plants that have taken minerals from the soil. In turn, when humans eat beef, we consume those same minerals. Humans need minerals such as potassium, magnesium, calcium and sodium, among many others, to stay healthy.

MARCEL TER BEKKE/GETTY IMAGES

Humans don't eat soil straight out of the ground, so we don't get our minerals and vitamins directly from it. But when we eat plants that were grown in the soil or meat and products such as milk from animals that ate plants grown in the soil, we indirectly take in all those good nutrients that our bodies need.

MIODRAG IGNJATOVIC/GETTY IMAGES

DIG IN DEEPER

X-rays Are an X-cellent Use of Soil Elements

A few years ago I slipped on an icy sidewalk and broke my wrist. I had to get an X-ray so that my doctor could see if I'd broken a bone. Tungsten is used in X-ray tubes. It's an element that's extracted by mining the soil. When an X-ray is taken, very small amounts of radiation pass through the body. The element terbium, also mined from soil, is used to limit the amount of radiation a patient is exposed to. It allows radiologists to take images quickly. When you have an MRI or a CT scan, you are also exposed to soil elements. Gadolinium is used to make the pictures taken during an MRI clearer and easier for doctors to read.

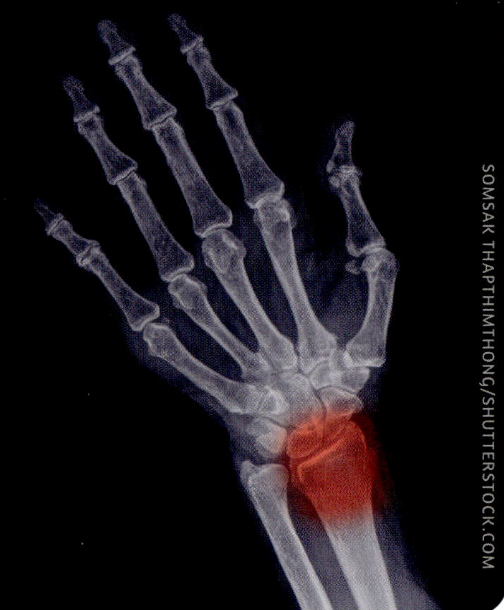

SOMSAK THAPTHIMTHONG/SHUTTERSTOCK.COM

SOIL IS NATURE'S KIDNEY

Soil texture also determines how ***groundwater*** is cleaned and filtered. Pockets of air in between soil particles allow water to move through soil. This is called soil porosity. As water moves through the soil, some contaminants in the water are removed and left in the soil. Some of the microorganisms in the soil can help decompose the contaminants and make them less dangerous. It's nature's way of cleaning itself—kind of like how our kidneys filter waste from our blood.

Water and soil have a unique relationship. One of the things soil can do is filter pollution and contaminants out of water.
RUUDMORIJN/GETTY IMAGES

JEAN-PHILIPPE TOURNUT/GETTY IMAGES

Living Inside the Earth

Earth houses are just that—houses made from earth! Since ancient times, houses like this have been built all over the world. There are several types of earth houses, many of which are still being constructed today. Adobe houses are common in the southwest United States and in the Middle East. They are built with bricks made by mixing soil with straw or grass. Rammed earth houses are made from sand that is pressed into forms. Compressed earth blocks made from clay, sand or lime are used to build some earth houses.

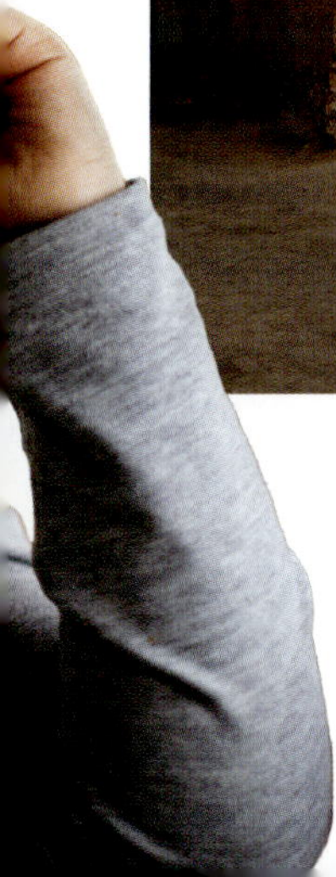

CHAPTER THREE

Soil Under Threat

Some human activity can harm the soil. Mining, large-scale agriculture and logging are just a few of the things we do that have a damaging impact on our soil as well as the health of organisms that rely on it to live. That includes us!

Growing only one crop, such as this rapeseed, in an area is called monoculture. Monocultures do not support a lot of different plant and animal species.

WONRY/GETTY IMAGES

THE STORY OF TAR CREEK

In 1891, in the Tar Creek area of Ottawa County, Oklahoma, miners began extracting zinc and lead ores from the earth. During the almost 70 years the mines were in operation, hundreds of pits, mine shafts and wells were dug. Some of the ores were removed from 385 feet (117 meters) below ground! At the peak of the mining operations in the area, 130,410 tons (118,305 tonnes) of lead and 749,254 tons (679, 711 tonnes) of zinc were removed and sent to smelters each year.

By the 1960s, low prices and decreased demand for metal stopped the operations at Tar Creek. The mines all closed. But nothing was done to clean up the area. ***Tailings*** ponds containing toxic wastes were left behind. Thousands of acres piled with materials left over from the extraction process were abandoned. Toxic heavy metals such as iron, cadmium, lead, nickel and zinc contaminated the soil. The acidic water from the wells and tailings ponds filtered into the groundwater, and eventually they ended up in Tar Creek. Fish, insects and other aquatic life in the creek died. The water was not safe to drink.

THE DAMAGE WAS DONE

Eventually, in the late 1970s, the government spent millions of dollars trying to clean up the site. Water wells were plugged so that contaminated water could no longer get into the soil and the groundwater. ***Remediation*** of mine wastes and soil started. But the damage was already done, and things didn't get better for the residents living nearby. Dozens of cave-ins due to unstable soil left from the mine tunnels made the area completely unsafe.

TOXIC

In North America, there are over 6,000 active landfills. Landfills are necessary. They contain waste that would otherwise be dumped into the environment. They keep communities from being dirty, unsanitary and unhealthy. But landfills are filled with pollutants such as lead, arsenic and petroleum products, which are toxic and can easily contaminate soil and groundwater. We can reduce the waste going into the landfill by making smarter choices when we are shopping and not buying things that are disposable. We can reuse or repurpose items. We can donate to charities things we don't want but that are still in good condition.

(MAIN) JENYA SMYK/SHUTTERSTOCK.COM; (INSET) ALEX PHOTOHUB/SHUTTERSTOCK.COM

The Tar Creek mining operations were closed in the 1960s, but the work to clean it up has never been finished.

OKLAHOMA DEPARTMENT OF ENVIRONMENTAL QUALITY

The town of Picher is no longer livable due to toxic waste left from the Tar Creek mining operation.
TIM DOWD/WIKIMEDIA COMMONS/CC BY 3.0

By the mid-1990s, tests revealed high ***concentrations*** of lead and cadmium in the soil in residential areas near the mines, including in a town called Picher. It was also discovered that the children living near the mine site had high concentrations of lead in their blood. Contaminated mine waste had been used to build roads, parking lots and driveways in the towns. Some residents chose to move out of the area and find new homes.

By 2009 the government had forced everyone in the town of Picher to leave, buying out their properties. Today Picher is a ghost town, and the site is still one of the most toxic places in the United States.

Partnering with Trees

Many chemicals are used when oil wells are drilled and oil is being extracted from them. Some chemicals make it easier to drill into the ground. Other chemicals increase the speed at which the oil flows out of the well. Some of these chemicals can contaminate the soil where the well is dug. The soil must be cleaned up before it is safe.

Researchers at the Northern Alberta Institute of Technology are exploring the idea of using lignochar to clean up oil well sites. Lignochar is made from tree lignin, which is found in the cells of trees. Lignin is what makes wood strong and helps hold it together. Lignin is left over when a tree is ***pulped*** to make paper, so it is easy to get. This also means that less of the wood is wasted. Researchers change the lignin into lignochar using high temperatures and high pressure. The cells in lignochar are very porous and can absorb some of the chemicals in contaminated soil at well sites.

SHERYL NORMANDEAU

RUSS HEINL/SHUTTERSTOCK.COM

Wildlife of all kinds is affected when rainforests are removed to grow palm trees for various commodities.
RICHCAREY/GETTY IMAGES

RAIGRJD/GETTY IMAGES

ARVIAN CAHYA WIRANATA/GETTY IMAGES

DEFORESTATION DEVASTATION

Palm oil is a common ingredient in food, and it is also used as ***biofuel***. Indonesia, Malaysia and Papua New Guinea produce up to 85 percent of all the palm oil in the world. By 2019 an estimated 9.1 million acres (3.7 million hectares) of rainforest were cut down in these three countries so that plantations could grow palm trees for biofuel. When so much of the natural forest is removed, numerous species of birds, insects and other wildlife lose their habitat and food sources. Cutting down multiple species of trees to plant only one type of tree means

To grow palm trees quickly in order to keep up with consumer demand, fertilizers and pesticides must be sprayed on them. These chemicals can contaminate both the soil the plants are growing in and nearby waterways.
SORI PADA PULUNGAN/SHUTTERSTOCK.COM

that ***biodiversity*** is lost. Forests store carbon dioxide, so that means deforestation increases global greenhouse gas emissions.

Deforestation also strips soil of its nutrients and moisture. The palm trees that are planted in place of the natural forest need a lot of fertilizer. They may also need ***pesticides*** to deal with problem insects. The overuse of chemicals means that the soil could become contaminated, and so could the groundwater. Depending on the pesticides used, beneficial insects could be killed along with the pests.

In 2019 the Indonesian government passed laws to prevent more palm plantations from being built in the country. Palm oil producers were also encouraged to restore some of the deforested land. As a result, fewer acres of land are now being used for palm oil production. In 2022 the Indonesian government began fining palm oil producers who were growing palm trees in protected forest areas. Roughly 494,210 acres (200,000 hectares) of forested land that was cleared for palm tree production will now be allowed to return to its natural state.

When deforestation occurs, animals such as these orangutans no longer have a place to live. They must move in order to find food and safe habitat.
ANUP SHAH/GETTY IMAGES

FIXING POLLUTED SOIL WITH PLANTS, FUNGI AND BACTERIA

Bioremediation is the practice of using plants, fungi or bacteria to clean up soil contaminated by heavy metals, such as lead or mercury, or organic contaminants, such as petroleum products. Researchers worldwide are studying the ways that oyster mushrooms (*Pleurotus ostreatus*) can clean up soil that has been polluted with cigarette butts, diesel oil and some types of plastic.

Plants such as chickweed and yarrow can be used to remove cadmium from soil. Other types of plants work to draw out other types of metals. This process is called phytoextraction. Scientists are still learning how bioremediation works, but it seems to have a promising future.

RISKI STYOBUDI/GETTY IMAGES

Plants and fungi are amazing! Researchers are experimenting with the use of oyster mushrooms and flowering plants such as yarrow to help remove heavy metals and contaminants from the soil.

TOMPET/SHUTTERSTOCK.COM

The excess mineral salts from fertilizer run off the soil when it rains. The salts eventually contaminate nearby rivers and streams. This harms our water supply and all the life in it.
SHERYL NORMANDEAU

THE PROBLEMS WITH LARGE-SCALE AGRICULTURE

Farmers need healthy soil to grow bumper crops of grains and other plants for people to eat. Unfortunately, large-scale ***conventional*** farming doesn't always focus on soil health. Some types of farm machinery and the way they are used harm the soil by compacting it or making it more likely to erode in wind or rain. Tilling the soil can hurt the organisms in the soil. When the balance is upset and the soil isn't healthy, more fertilizers are needed to ***replenish*** the nutrients. Too much fertilizer can run off into the soil and then into the groundwater. It may eventually end up in a river or lake and cause problems such as algae blooms.

Algae blooms reduce the amount of oxygen in the water and can be bad for fish and other aquatic animals. Fertilizer runoff can also cause too many weeds to grow in lakes that are near farms. Weeds can choke out other plants in the water. They can also keep sunlight from reaching animals and other plants in the water. It's not just about how too much fertilizer affects soil and water. Fertilizer produces greenhouse gases such as nitrogen oxides, so it affects the atmosphere too.

Regenerative farming and gardening techniques can help make harvests more bountiful and sustainable.
JEANNY TSAI/GETTY IMAGES

BETTER FARMING TECHNIQUES TO THE RESCUE

Some farmers are using ***regenerative*** farming techniques to restore the health of the soil and make sure it is full of life well into the future. Techniques include using fewer pesticides (or none at all), avoiding overfertilizing and deep tilling, and reducing soil ***compaction*** by not running heavy machinery on fields unless it's absolutely necessary. We can do some of the same things in our gardens!

Crop rotation is another technique that boosts soil health. It means changing the kind of crop planted in a field, not planting the same type every single year. Many gardeners do this too. There are a few reasons why this is a good idea. Not all plants have the same type of root system. Some have deep tap roots, and others have roots that spread sideways as well as down. Putting plants with different root systems in fields from year to year makes the soil better. It will be less compacted. It will be more porous and allow more water and air to pass through. Plants will grow better.

Another reason why crop rotation is useful is that some plants attract specific types of insects. For example, kale and cabbage are commonly attacked by flea beetles. Replacing the kale and cabbage one year with tomatoes, which flea beetles don't like, will encourage the flea beetles to move on. This approach can wipe out cycles of insect infestations.

Insect pests can threaten the health of plants. This leafy vegetable isn't so edible anymore after the flea beetles got to it!
I III II I III II I/SHUTTERSTOCK

Drone Detectives in the Field

Drones are used in agriculture around the world to monitor such things as soil conditions and crop growth. Drones are equipped with ***high-resolution*** cameras that can track what is happening in the field below them. The cameras record information like what types of weeds are growing, what pests are attacking the plants and if the soil is too wet or too dry. The farmer uses this data to decide whether to fertilize the field, use more (or less) ***irrigation*** or apply a herbicide or insecticide to a specific area. This can reduce costs, and because only spot treatments are done, excess fertilizer and other chemicals are not added to the soil and groundwater. Another huge benefit of using a drone to fly over a field is that the field can be observed without compacting the soil by using a heavy vehicle or machine.

GOCE/GETTY IMAGES

Imagine if all the soil in the world looked like this. How would we grow our food?

PIYASET/GETTY IMAGES

DEVASTATING DESERTIFICATION

Desertification happens when land that was once able to grow food is destroyed by drought, erosion, poor agricultural practices and deforestation. The soil becomes desert-like. It is dry and without nutrients. It does not support the organisms that make up the soil food web. This threatens the food supply for humans as well as wildlife. Social problems such as poverty, poor health and a lack of clean drinking water are worsened by desertification. According to the United Nations, 500 million people currently live in areas that have experienced desertification over the last 45 years.

The Dust Bowl

In the 1930s much of the United States and Canada was affected by severe drought. Areas such as the Great Plains region of the United States turned into what became known as a dust bowl, due to the massive dust storms that frequently occurred. High winds scooped topsoil from the fields and blasted it into the air.

Many factors contributed to what's called the Dirty Thirties. The effects of World War I and the Great Depression had left many people poor and unemployed. Acres of grassland had been replaced with wheat crops to meet increased demand during the war. When prices for those crops dropped, the land was left without native vegetation to hold topsoil in place. Farmers went into debt buying new equipment and more land. Some of the equipment they were using, such as one-way disk plows, were not good for the soil. They were fast and could till a lot of land in a short time, but they damaged the soil by breaking up the particles in it and disturbing the microorganisms living there. Years of severe drought meant that the soil simply turned into dust. It had no nutrients in it. Crops could not grow.

DOROTHEA LANGE/WIKIMEDIA COMMONS/PUBLIC DOMAIN

LIBRARY OF CONGRESS, PRINTS & PHOTOGRAPHS DIVISION, FARM SECURITY ADMINISTRATION/OFFICE OF WAR INFORMATION BLACK-AND-WHITE NEGATIVES

Natural disasters such as flooding and wildfire can critically affect soil and the organisms that rely on it.
SCARORA/GETTY IMAGES

JANET MELROSE

DESIGN PICS/BLAKE KENT/GETTY IMAGES

ENVIRONMENTAL DAMAGE

The impacts of severe weather and natural disasters on soil are huge. Flooding, wildfires, wind and drought can all cause changes in the amount of nutrients found in the soil. Plant and animal life is affected, and the many different microorganisms that live in the soil. Crop growth and quality can be compromised. Extreme weather events can have big consequences for human food sources too. Soil movement happens when flooding causes runoff. Sometimes pollutants are transported into soil when an area is flooded. High winds may erode the soil and blow it into other areas.

Wildfires burn away all the vegetation growing in the soil. Until new plants grow back, there are no roots to hold the soil together. The soil is bare. If there are heavy rains or strong winds, the soil will erode. If the area is on a slope, landslides may occur.

Fire isn't always bad! Sometimes forestry management teams perform controlled burns. These are fires that are set and kept under control by firefighters. They are not as hot and damaging as wildfires. Controlled burns are often used to reduce the amount of fuel that has built up in a forest—trees that have been damaged by pests or diseases. Removing fuel from an area helps keep wildfires from getting out of control and threatening areas where humans live. After a controlled burn, new plants will grow and keep the soil from eroding away. Ash from controlled burns covers the soil and can also prevent some soil erosion.

CHAPTER FOUR

Healthy Soil for the Future

Giving our soil a healthy boost doesn't have to be hard or take a lot of time. From growing a garden to making compost, you can make a positive difference in the quality of the soil around us!

One of the best ways to protect our soil is to make sure there are plants growing in it.
MAYUR KAKADE/GETTY IMAGES

PLANTING FOR CHANGE

What is one of the best ways we can make our soil healthier? Grow plants! Planted soil doesn't erode as easily as bare soil. All those roots help keep the soil in place. Fill your garden with as many different types of plants as you can. Plants that grow naturally in your region and are not introduced from another part of the world are called native. These are good plants to attract birds and other wildlife to your garden. Pollinator insects will enjoy visiting bountiful blooms. Think of your garden as an ***ecosystem***, inviting all sorts of living organisms to eat, reproduce and make their homes there.

PUT A LIVING BLANKET OVER THE SOIL

You can boost your garden soil's health by planting cover crops. This is just what it sounds like. Cover crops are plants that are grown in the garden during times when there are no other ones growing. For example, you might be growing vegetables in the spring and summer, but you aren't growing anything in the fall. You can plant a cover crop to keep the soil from being left bare. Cover crops usually grow very quickly from seed. They include peas, buckwheat, rye, alfalfa and winter wheat. Before you plant more vegetables in the spring, you can cut down the cover crops and add them to the soil. They will decompose and leave nutrients in the soil for your new plants to use. It's like composting right there in the garden instead of in a bin!

Let's Celebrate Soil!

The United Nations celebrates World Soil Day every year on December 5. It is a day to recognize how important soil is to life on Earth and learn what we can do to protect it. On this day events are held all over the world to educate people about soil conservation. There are several ways you can celebrate World Soil Day. You could hold a poster contest at your school to raise awareness. Or maybe do some fun experiments, like testing the pH of soil samples from your school garden. You could also volunteer to help make compost at a nearby community garden.

Big garden or small garden, it doesn't matter! Growing some of your own food is a fun, rewarding experience—plus, you get to eat everything after you harvest!
JANET MELROSE

NICK DAVID/GETTY IMAGES

SHERYL NORMANDEAU

Putting compost in your soil is one of the best ways you can boost its health! All that decomposed organic matter gives the soil nutrients and makes your plants grow better.

COMPOST COMPOSITION

Put fruit and vegetable scraps, a bunch of dried leaves, some twigs from trees that were just pruned, a handful of coffee grounds, some eggshells and a pile of grass clippings together in a big bin and let them be, and they will all decompose. Eventually you'll get compost.

Compost is a type of soil amendment—something added to the soil to improve it. Compost contains nutrients that plants can use. It can make your soil easier to cultivate and work with. Compost also increases the amount of moisture your soil can hold. Amending your soil with compost is an all-around good idea!

Compost can be made in many ways. The method just described is called cold, or ***passive***, composting. It's easier to do than hot composting, which is done by mixing the ingredients of the compost so that the temperature of the mixture is very high. The mixture must be stirred frequently to allow oxygen to help break down the pile faster. Sometimes you need to add water to help the decomposition process.

Cold composting doesn't require you to turn the ingredients. You just put all the waste into a bin and let it rot over time. It is a much slower method than hot composting, but it works! This is the type of composting most people do in their gardens. Let time, water and oxygen do the job!

COMPOST THIS!

Store-bought compost bins are usually made of heavy-duty plastic, wood or wire. At my community garden, we constructed compost bins using recycled wood pallets that a department store was going to throw out. We used wire to attach the pallets together. Two of the bins are for plant waste such as dead leaves and twigs, and the third bin holds the finished compost. Our pallet system allows plenty of air to get into the bins and help the decomposition process. The size of the bins makes it easy for us to turn (mix) the compost every week. If we don't get rain for a long time, we water the decaying material in the bins so that it breaks down more quickly. Hot, damp conditions are ideal for decomposition.

After several months, our third bin is filled with rich black compost. In the spring, all the gardeners add a bit to their garden beds. The compost improves the soil and gives some nutrients to the plants throughout the season.

Put Worms to Work!

A vermicomposter is a special type of compost system in which earthworms do the work of breaking down food scraps. Worms called red wigglers (*Eisenia fetida*) are placed inside a bin along with some damp bedding. I give my worms food waste such as carrot and potato peels, apple cores and banana peels. As they eat the food, they excrete castings (poop). The castings have nutrients in them that my plants can use to grow.

SHERYL NORMANDEAU

Bison can contribute to soil health.
ROB NORMANDEAU

Learning to garden is a good way for generations to connect!
ANDRESR/GETTY IMAGES

THE STORY OF COMPOSTING WITH BISON

A large herd of more than 300 bison lives on 1,198 acres (485 hectares) of Tsuut'ina Nation reserve land in southwestern Alberta. Bison (or buffalo as they are also known) are a traditional food as well as a textile and tool source for Indigenous Peoples in the prairie and woodland areas of central North America. Some of the bison in the Tsuut'ina's herd are used for food by residents, but the bison are also raised to help the Tsuut'ina keep their connection to their rich cultural traditions.

The way bison graze is good for soil health. As they walk through the land they graze on they trample some of the plants, which decompose and produce compost. The nutrients that are in the compost help other plants that grow on the land. The bison also produce a smelly but helpful side benefit! Some of the waste the bison create is composted and used to enrich the soil in the Tsuut'ina Nation's community garden. (Because the waste is left to decompose for a long time before it is used in the garden, it loses its stinky odor.) Vegetable and fruit scraps from the school also give the compost pile a boost. When food is grown in the garden for the residents to eat, the cycle is complete. Everything is part of the natural, sustainable system.

TRACK THE SMAP

Become a ***citizen scientist***! Help researchers conserve soil through various projects that can be done at home and at school. The Soil Moisture Active Passive (SMAP) is a mission started in 2015 by NASA (National Aeronautics and Space Administration). A satellite orbited Earth on a three-year mission to measure the moisture content of soil on Earth (except for the soil covered in water or ice). Scientists use data gathered by SMAP to track how the climate is changing on a global scale. After the mission ended in 2018, the SMAP satellite was put to use gathering data about agricultural soils. As part of the Global Learning and Observations to Benefit the Environment Program (GLOBE), students in schools around the world can participate in the SMAP program by taking soil-moisture samples on the ground. The information collected by students can help farmers make decisions about water use.

Keep the World Beautiful

In 1953 a group of community and business leaders in New York started the Keep America Beautiful campaign. Their goal was to convince Americans that cleaning up litter was a way to show some pride and respect for the entire country. Volunteers from all over the nation joined the campaign, and each year they participated in various events to clean up parks, ditches, waterways and highways. In the 1990s Keep America Beautiful started encouraging citizens, including kids, to recycle what they could. The Keep America Beautiful organization is still working in many states today. Their efforts help keep soil from being polluted.

More ways to keep our soil healthy include contributing to citizen-science projects such as SMAP and participating in community cleanup projects. Big or small, it all matters!

NASA/PUBLIC DOMAIN

CATHERINE FALLS COMMERCIAL/GETTY IMAGES

CHORES TO SAVE THE SOIL

Whether you are washing the family car or mowing the lawn, you can help keep chemicals out of the soil. When you wash your vehicle at home, everything from detergents to fuel residue and motor oil pours into the soil. It filters into the groundwater and eventually reaches rivers and streams. This harms both soil and aquatic life. Choose to clean the car at a car wash instead—they have drains that go directly to urban water-treatment plants. When you mow the lawn, make sure you don't spill oil or fuel onto the soil. The best solution is to use either an electric mower or a reel mower that runs on just your push power. If you are painting a fence or a shed, don't allow any paint, thinner or cleaner to come into contact with the soil. Before you do any chores outside, think about the potential risk for polluting the soil and how you might get the job done in a different, safer way.

ELVIS901/GETTY IMAGES

Everything counts! Reducing our use of chemicals and storing and disposing of them properly makes a big difference to soil and water health. We can make a conscious decision to change the ways we look after our gardens and lawns to care for our soil.
MICHAEL BERMAN/GETTY IMAGES

SHERYL NORMANDEAU

ROB NORMANDEAU

It's all part of the cycle! Bees and other pollinators love plants that grow in healthy soil!

YASSER CHALID/GETTY IMAGES

The Great Global Cleanup

Each year on Earth Day (April 22), people around the world join the Great Global Cleanup. This event focuses on raising awareness of plastic waste and how much damage it does to the environment, but it is also a time to clean up garbage. You can see a map of where all the Great Global Cleanup events are happening at earthday.org. If you like to organize and plan, maybe you could create a cleanup event in your school or community!

FOUNDATION FOR THE FUTURE

Soil takes thousands of years to form, but it can be destroyed in a very short time by human activity and natural disasters. Yet soil is vital to all life. When I visit my plot in the community garden, I can see evidence of the soil food web in action. If I dig just a little bit below the surface of the soil, I find earthworms. Vegetables and flowers are rooted firmly in the soil, and I know that soon there will be tomatoes and cucumbers for me to harvest. Bumblebees zip around the flowers and collect pollen. There are voles living in nooks and crannies beneath the compost bins, and magpies dart down from the sky to scoop up grubs from the soil. I want to keep this soil story going. I hope you do too!

Acknowledgments

There are not enough words to convey my thanks to the massively talented publishing team at Orca Book Publishers!

All my love goes out to my husband, Rob, my mum and dad and my brother Derek.

A huge thank-you to Rob Normandeau, Tina Boisvert and Janet Melrose, who contributed images to the book.

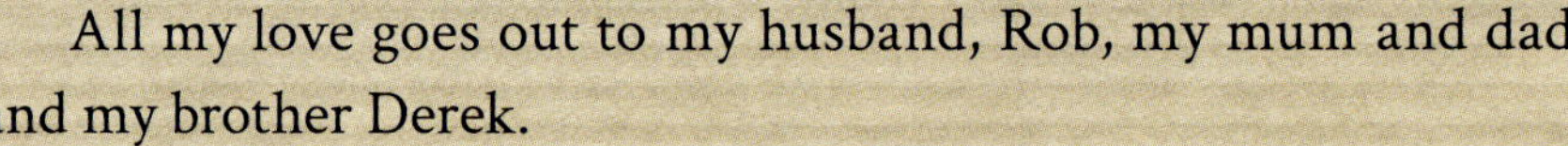

YAKOBCHUKOLENA/GETTY IMAGES

Resources

Print

Bowman, Chris. *Soil.* Bellwether Media, 2014.
Gardner, Robert. *Science Fair Projects About Water and Soil.* Enslow Publishing, 2017.
Huddleston, Emma. *Looking at Layers: Looking into Soil.* Child's World, 2020.
Lawrence, Ellen. *Dirt.* Bearport Publishing, 2013.
Lowe, Lindsey. *Outdoor Science Lab: Life in the Soil.* PowerKids Press, 2020.
MacAulay, Kelley. *Why Do We Need Soil?* Crabtree Publishing, 2014.
Murray, Laura K. *Why Do We Need Soil?* Pebble Books, 2023.
Peterson, Cris. *Seed, Soil, Sun: Earth's Recipe for Food.* Boyds Mill Press, 2012.
Schuh, Mari. *Soil Basics.* Capstone Press, 2011.
Stroud, Dr. Jackie. *Under Your Feet: Soil, Sand, and Everything Underground.* DK Children, 2020.

Online

Canadian Soil Information Service: sis.agr.gc.ca/cansis

Kids Gardening (All the Dirt on Soil):
kidsgardening.org/resources/gardening-basics-all-the-dirt-on-soil

Soil Conservation Council of Canada: soilcc.ca

Soil Science Society of America: soils.org

Soils 4 Kids: soils4kids.org

Soils of Canada: soilsofcanada.ca

World Soil Day (Food and Agriculture Organization of the United Nations):
fao.org/world-soil-day/en

GMVOZD/GETTY IMAGES

Glossary

antibiotic—a medicine that kills or slows down infections caused by bacteria

archaeologists—people who study human history by digging through historical sites and looking for artifacts

beneficial—producing good results

biodiversity—the variety of life in an environment

biofuel—fuel made out of plant or animal waste

citizen scientist— a person who is not trained as a scientist but helps gather data for a scientific organization

clinical trials—studies done to be sure a drug works and is safe for humans to use

compaction—the action of pressing together. Compaction of soil forces air out of the soil particles.

concentrations—the amounts of something in a given area or volume

conventional—normal, usual

crop rotation—the practice of planting different crops on the same land in sequence

crustaceans—invertebrate animals that have a hard body covering called an exoskeleton

ecosystem—all the living and nonliving things in an area, such as animals, plants, rocks and water

eroded—worn down

extracted—removed

greenhouse gases—gases in Earth's atmosphere that trap heat

groundwater—water that is stored beneath the ground surface

high-resolution—describes an image that is extremely clear and of excellent quality

irrigation—the watering of land

mutate—to change, often negatively

paleontologists—people who study the history of animal life by digging up fossils

passive—not active, inert

pesticides—chemicals used to control or treat pests

pharmaceutical—a medicinal drug

photosynthesize—to convert energy from light into sugars

pulped—chopped into pieces and reduced to pulp

regenerative—tending to restore or renew something, such as the health of the soil in a garden or field

remediation—the act of repairing or cleaning up

replenish—fill or build up again

resistant—not harmed by or affected by something

tailings—waste left over from a process such as mining

Index

Page numbers in **bold** *indicate an image caption.*

RANDALL ALLCOCK

SHERYL NORMANDEAU is a lifelong gardener and holds a Prairie Horticulture Certificate and a Sustainable Urban Agriculture Certificate. She is a freelance writer specializing in gardening writing, with hundreds of articles published. Sheryl is a regular contributor to *The Gardener for Canadian Climates* and *The Prairie Garden*, and she is the author of *Save Our Seeds: Protecting Plants for the Future* and *The Little Prairie Book of Berries*. She lives in Calgary.